FOREST
ECHO

FOREST ECHO

by G.A. SKREBITSKI

*Translated from the Russian
by Anne Terry White*

A VENTURE BOOK · GEORGE BRAZILLER · NEW YORK

Translation copyright © 1967 by Anne Terry White
Original illustrations copyright © 1967 by George Braziller, Inc.

All rights in this book are reserved.
For information, address the publisher:
George Braziller, Inc.
One Park Avenue, New York, New York 10016

Library of Congress Catalog Card Number: 66–21974

First Printing

Designed by Hilda Scott

Printed in the United States of America

Contents

FOREST ECHO 1

HUNTING BLACKCOCK 10

BIRTHDAY 15

THE TOMTIT 29

A PRESENT 38

A THOUGHTFUL MAMMA 46

BABY STORKS 50

LONGEARS 57

THE DRAW 63

MY FIRST TROPHY 68

Forest Echo

"What title do you want to give to your collection of stories?" the editor asked me.

I began to ponder. To think up a title for a book isn't an easy job. The title should reflect the very heart of a book, the main thing the author wants to pass on to the reader.

What, then, do I want to tell boys and girls about?

I want to tell them about my wanderings as a hunter in the forest and on the marsh, about how from childhood I learned to understand and love nature. I want to awaken this interest and love in my readers, too.

So what should I call my book? I thought about the title and at the same time I thought: "Which of my first impressions in the forest do I remember most vividly?"

And I remembered a little incident that happened in my earliest childhood.

I was then five or six years old. We lived in the country.

Once Mamma went to the forest to pick wild strawberries and took me with her. That year there was a very good crop of wild strawberries. They grew just behind the village, in an old forest clearing.

I recall that day as if it were now, although more than forty years have passed since then. It was a summer day, sunny-hot. But we no sooner got to the forest than suddenly a dark cloud appeared and out of it poured fast, heavy rain. Yet the sun still continued to shine. The rain fell on the ground, splashing hard against the leaves. The drops hung on the grass, on the branches of bushes and trees, and the sun played on each drop and was reflected in it.

Mamma and I had scarcely got under a tree when the sun shower was already over.

"Look, Ura, how lovely!" said Mamma, coming out from under the branches.

I looked up. Across the whole sky a many-colored rainbow stretched in an arc. One end rested against our village, while the other went far off to the meadows beyond the river.

"It's fine," said I. "Just like a bridge. If only we could run on it!"

Mamma laughed and led me into a glade where everywhere, by hummocks and stumps, we found big, ripe berries.

From the sun-heated earth, a light vapor rose after the rain. The air smelled of flowers, honey, and strawberries. You sniffed this wonderful smell—it was just as if you had swallowed some sort of fragrant, sweet drink. And to make it more so, I picked strawberries and put them not into my basket, but straight into my mouth.

I ran from bush to bush, shaking off the last drops of rain. Then a big yellow butterfly flew over the glade. I snatched off my cap and raced after it. But the butterfly now came down right to the grass, now rose up high. I chased and chased but didn't catch it—it flew off somewhere into the forest.

All panting, I stopped and looked around. Where was Mamma? I couldn't see her anywhere.

"Ah-ooh!" I shouted, the way I shouted when playing hide-and-seek near the house.

And suddenly from somewhere far off, from the depths of the forest I heard an answering "Ah-ooh!"

I was startled. Had I really run so far away from Mamma? Where was she? How would I find her? The whole forest, so gay before, now seemed mysterious, frightening.

"Mamma! Mamma!" I yelled with all my might, ready to burst into tears.

"A-ma-ma-ma-ma-a-a-a!" someone far off seemed to mock me. And that very second Mamma ran out from the nearby bushes.

"Why are you shouting? What happened?" she asked, frightened.

"I thought you were far away!" I answered, calmed at once. "Somebody in the forest is mocking."

"Who is mocking?" Mamma didn't understand.

"I don't know. I shout—and he shouts, too. Just listen!" And again, but bravely now, I shouted:

"Ah-ooh! Ah-ooh!"

"Ah-ooh! Ah-ooh! Ah-ooh!" came an answer from the forest distance.

"Why, that's the echo!" said Mamma.

"Echo? And what's it doing there?"

"Not doing anything. Your own voice is given back in the forest, and to you it seems that someone is answering you."

I listened to Mamma doubtfully. How could it be my own voice that answered me when I was already silent?

Again I tried shouting:

"Come here!"

"Here-ere-ere!" came the answer in the forest.

"Mamma, but can't it be that someone really is mocking?" I asked hesitantly. "Let's go and look."

"What a silly you are!" laughed Mamma. "Well, let's go if you want to, but we won't find anyone."

I took hold of Mamma's hand, just in case. "Who knows what this echo is!" I thought. And we walked along the path into the depths of the forest. Now and then I shouted:

"Are you here?"

"Here-ere-ere!" something answered up ahead.

We crossed the forest ravine and came out into a light little birch grove. Here it wasn't at all terrifying. I let go of Mamma's hand and ran on.

And suddenly I saw "echo." It was sitting on a stump with its back to me. It was all gray, in a gray, shaggy hat, like a wood goblin in a fairy-tale picture. I cried out and dashed back to Mamma.

"Mamma, Mamma, there's echo sitting on a stump!"

"Why do you keep saying foolish things?" Mamma said, growing angry.

She took me by the hand again and went forward bravely.

"But it won't touch us, will it?" I asked.

"Don't be foolish, please," answered Mamma.

We came out on a glade.

"There, over there!" I whispered.

"But that's Grandfather Kuzma pasturing the cows!"

Hearing Mamma's voice, "echo" turned around, and I saw the familiar white beard, mustache, and eyebrows that looked like cotton batting glued just for fun to the sunburned face, wrinkled as a baked apple.

"Grandfather, I though you were echo!" I cried, running up to the old man.

"Echo?" he said in surprise, putting down the little wooden shepherd's pipe he was whittling with his knife. "Echo—that, dear one, is not a person. That's the forest voice."

"Forest voice?" I didn't understand.

"It's like this. You shout in the forest, and it answers you. Every tree, every bush gives back the sound. Just

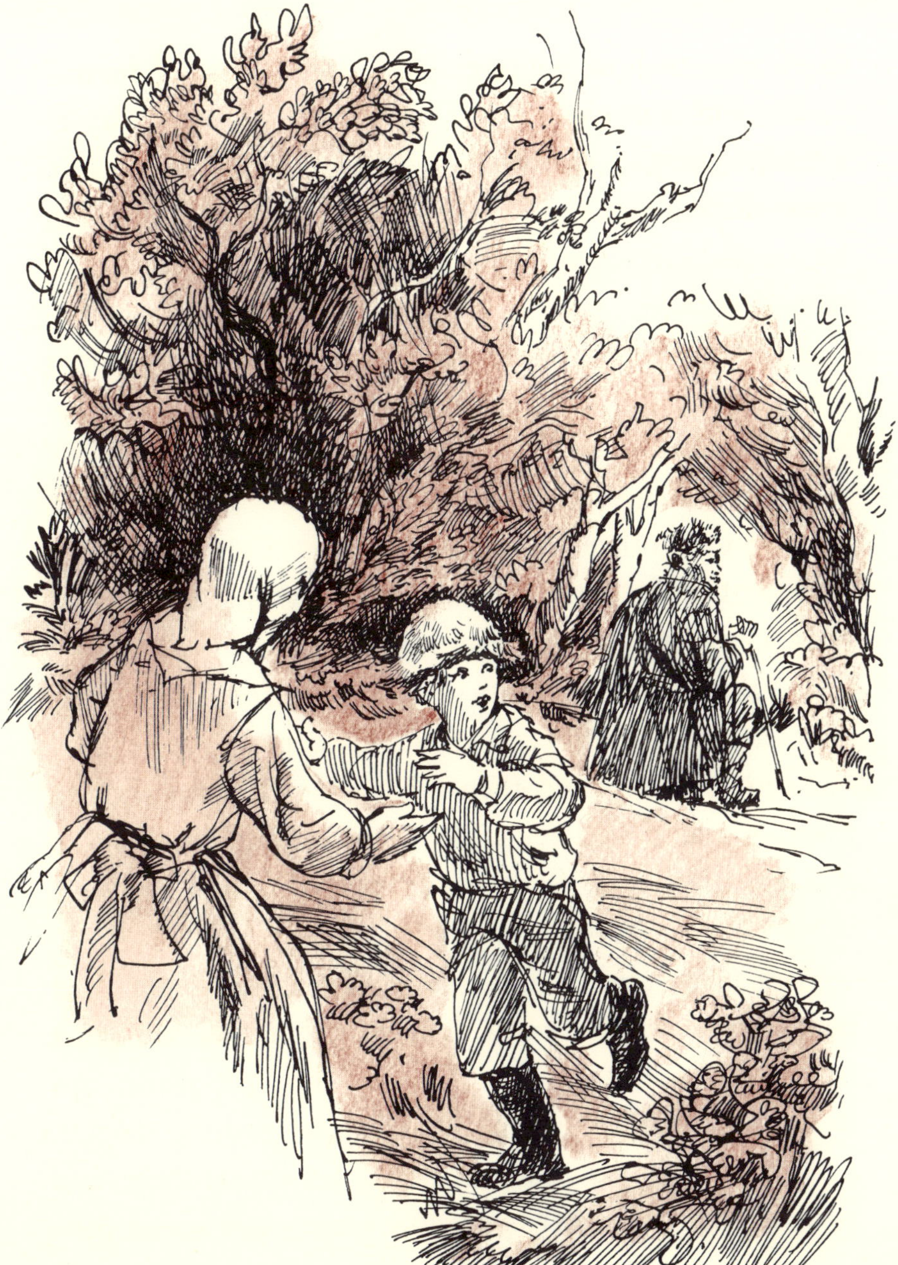

listen now to how we're going to talk back and forth."

The old man picked up his pipe and began to play in a tender, long-drawn-out way. He played just as if he were singing some sad little song. And somewhere far, far in the forest, another voice just like it took up the second part.

Mamma came up and sat down on a neighboring stump. Grandfather finished playing, and the echo finished, too.

"There, sonny, now you've heard how the forest and I call to each other," said the old man. "Echo—that's the very soul of the forest. What the bird whistles, what the beast cries—it will pass everything on to you, it won't hide a thing. And you just go along the forest and listen to it. It will reveal to you all the mystery of the forest."

I didn't understand then what the echo was. But to make up for that, I fell in love with it for life—I loved it as the mysterious forest voice, as the song of the pipe, as an old childhood fairy tale.

And now, after many, many years, no sooner do I hear the echo in the forest than at once it all comes back to me: the sunny day, the birches, the little glade, and in the middle of it, on an old stump, something shaggy, gray. Perhaps it is our village herdsman sitting there, and perhaps it isn't the herdsman but a fairy-tale wood goblin. He sits on a stump, whittling a maplewood pipe. And then he will play on it in the quiet evening hour when trees, grass, and flowers fall asleep, and the horned moon slowly moves out from behind the forest, and the summer night comes on.

Forest echo—that is one of my very earliest and most vivid memories of the forest. So let my book of stories be called that.

I want these stories to be at least a faint echo of the life of nature in my homeland. I hope that, like the echo, they will entice boys and girls to peep into the wild, mysterious forest depths.

Hunting Blackcock

My father was a doctor, but at heart he was a fisherman and hunter. In his study hung guns, a cartridge belt, a game bag. And in the corner stood fishing rods, a pail, a folding stool, and other fishing things.

I was continually going into Papa's study. I would look all these remarkable things over for a long time, and dream that when I grew up, I also would certainly become a fisherman and hunter.

We lived on the very edge of the village, and right behind it began a young birch forest. In the summertime we youngsters used to lose ourselves there whole days at a time.

You'd go along a forest path—birches and hazelnut bushes all around. The sun showed through the green branches and scattered itself on the ground in a thousand golden circles. And you stepped along the path strewn with sun-gold and looked to the sides, under the bushes—maybe a pot-bellied white mushroom was hiding by a stump.

And in the fall I would go hunting in the forest. Instead of a gun, I took a stick, and I roamed in the forest, imagining that I was tracking a wild beast. I'd see an old moss-covered stump—and imagine to myself that it was a bear. Even I myself got terrified. I'd fire my stick-gun, snatch a wooden dagger out of my belt, and go into hand-to-hand combat with the beast. . . .

Mornings in late autumn, blackcock used to fly to the edge of the forest. They would spread over the birches and, seated on slender branches, would nip off birch catkins and feed on them.

I tried to get up as early as possible and run out on the mound to feast my eyes on these big black birds. But not once did I succeed in stealing up closer to them.

I'd just start to steal up, but the blackcock would already have noticed me and stretched out their long necks, on the alert. I'd take another step or two, they would flap-flap their wings—and off they'd fly.

But once it happened that the forester, Grandfather Ivan, dropped in on my father. I told him how I ran out mornings to look at the blackcock but could never manage to steal up to them. Grandfather laughed and said:

"Well, we'll outsmart them! Ask Father to let you go hunting with me tomorrow. But don't you oversleep, now!"

That night I woke up every minute—I was afraid all the time I'd oversleep. Grandfather came after me when it was still quite dark, and long before daylight we were already making our way along the forest path. The old man carried a gun and a bag on his back. I asked:

"Grandfather, what's in your bag?"

But he only waved his hand as if to say: "When the time comes, you'll see."

We came out on a glade. A blind was standing there. The old man laid his gun on the ground and untied his bag. I looked in and simply gasped. In the bag lay two blackcock made from rags—a hen out of gaily colored rags and a rooster out of black ones. The rooster's tail was made of real blackcock feathers. I couldn't in the least understand what Grandfather wanted these toy birds for, but he kept smiling and said nothing to my questions. He chopped off two long poles, fixed the rag birds on top, and leaned the poles against a birch tree in the center of the glade. From a distance you'd think that two real live blackcock were sitting on the birch.

Grandfather crawled into the blind and called me to him.

"Listen," he said to me, "when it is quite light, the blackcock will fly out on the glade to feed. They will see our birds—they'll think those are live ones and will sit down by them to nip off the birch buds together. And then we will shoot them."

I sat down more comfortably, spread the branches of the blind a little, and looked outside. In the forest it was somehow bleak, uninviting. The trees had lost their leaves, stood blackened, bare, while on the ground lay a white prickly hoarfrost. No birds' voices could be heard —only fluffy little tomtits cheeped, flying from branch to branch.

But now the sun appeared over the forest. The hoarfrost began to melt, to gleam with many-colored lights, and the whole forest at once grew more cheerful, filled with the rosy morning light.

Suddenly, somewhere quite near, I heard the noise of wings: a big bird was flying! I looked through a gap— on our birch tree, right beside our rag birds, I saw a real live blackcock sitting down, and what a big, beautiful one! Never once had I seen a blackcock so close. You could make out each feather. He was all black, with a bluish cast. The tail feathers curled to either side, and over his eyes were red brows. He sat down on the branch, raised his head, and looked around.

Suddenly I shouted:

"Fire, Grandfather, fire!"

The blackcock took fright and flew away.

And Grandfather got very angry.

"Is it allowed," he said, "to shout on a hunt? Now you've frightened all the blackcock. All for nothing I took you with me!"

So that time we didn't shoot anything.

Birthday

Once late in the evening, after I had had my fill of running in the yard, I was sitting with Papa and Mamma at the table. We were having supper.

"Do you know what day is tomorrow?" asked Mamma.

"I know—Sunday," I answered.

"Right. But besides that, tomorrow is your birthday. You are going to be eight years old."

"Oho, but he has grown very big already!" said Papa, as if surprised by it. "Eight years . . . that's no joke. In the fall he will go to school. What shall we give him for a present on such a day?"

"I myself don't know," Mamma replied, smiling. "We'll have to think of something."

I sat as if on pins and needles, listening to this conversation. Of course, Papa and Mamma were just teasing when they said they didn't know what to give me. A present had really been prepared long ago. But what kind of present?

I knew that no matter how much I asked, not for anything would either Papa or Mamma tell me before tomorrow. I had to wait.

After supper I went right to bed so that tomorrow should come sooner. But to fall asleep proved not so simple. Thoughts about the present kept creeping into my head, and in spite of myself I listened to what Papa and Mamma were saying in the next room. Perhaps, thinking that I was already asleep, they would say something about the present. But they were talking about something else. So, having heard nothing, I finally fell asleep.

In the morning, as soon as I woke up, I jumped at once from my bed and was about to run for my present. But I didn't need to run anywhere—by the wall near my bed stood two new, little, folding fishing rods, and there also, on a nail, hung a little pail for fish, painted green, with a cover, just like Papa's, only smaller.

I clapped my hands for joy. Jumping up on the bed, I began to dress as fast as I could.

While I was doing this, the door opened and into my room came Papa and Mamma, gay and smiling.

"Well, we congratulate you! Is the present good? Are

you pleased?" asked Papa. "Those are real fishing rods, not like your sticks and strings. With such a rod you can pull out even a pike."

"Very, very pleased!" I said happily. "Only where will I catch pike with them? In our river there aren't any, and you don't take me fishing with you—you say I'm too little yet."

"Well, I didn't take you before," replied Papa, "when you were only seven. But now you are already eight. To my thinking you grew a lot in just one night. How enormous he is!"

"Today we are all going together to catch fish," Mamma said merrily. "Wash yourself quickly, drink your tea, and we'll go. The weather is marvelous."

I ate my breakfast as fast as I could, grabbed my fishing rods and pail, and ran outside. By the stoop there already stood a horse harnessed to a small cart. Papa and Mamma put in our fishing rods, a teapot, kettle, and a bag of provisions, and we started on our journey.

When we had ridden beyond the village, Papa gave me the reins and said:

"Drive—you aren't little any more now, you know. And I will smoke a bit meanwhile."

I took the reins in my hands with joy. But to drive the horse, as a matter of fact, wasn't necessary. The road didn't turn off anywhere, but went perfectly straight between fields of rye.

The rye was already in ear, and over it sailed light shadows from the clouds.

Our horse ran merrily along. Now and then larks flew up from the road in front, and flying a little way off, sat down on the ground again.

We passed through a birch wood and came out on the river.

Right on its bank was a water mill. At this point the

river was dammed up by a dike and spread out into a wide pond.

We left our horse in the mill yard, took our fishing rods and pails out of the cart, and went off to fish.

Below the dam there was a deep millpool. We went down to it and sat down on the bank in a glade between green willow bushes.

To the right of us rose the dam, which held back the whole mass of water. The water tore through the cracks in the dam, gushed out with a loud noise in powerful fountains, and fell into the pool.

And on the other bank of the pool stood the old water mill. It was a rather small wooden house. One of its walls came right to the water, and fastened to the wall were two enormous paddle wheels, also of wood, like on a ship. Their lower edges dipped in the water.

The walls, the posts, thick as trees, that held up the wheels—everything was covered with green water-plants. They hung down right to the water, like long beards.

Suddenly the huge wheels shook and began to turn. At first slowly, then faster and faster, and with noise and splash, whole floods of water began to flow down. The water under the wheels foamed as if it were boiling and ran through the pool and farther, down the river, in a seething, boiling flood.

I was seeing all this for the first time in my life and couldn't tear my eyes from the wonderful sight.

On account of the powerful turning of the wheels, the whole mill shook, and it seemed to me that any moment it would start from its place and sail down the river like a ship.

"It's a good thing the mill has begun to work," said Papa. "The water has moved from under the wheels. At such a time the fish are more lively and rise to the bait better. Put on a worm quick as you can. Start catching."

We unwound our rods and cast. In the little cove near our bank the water, shut in by osier bushes, was calm.

I sat beside Papa and attentively looked at the floats. They lay still on top of the water. Some sort of little mosquitoes and midges crowded merrily in the air over the floats, constantly sitting down on them and flying up anew.

But now the float of my fishing rod seemed to come to life. It stirred slightly, making rings in the water around itself. It moved again and once more, then started slowly to dip in the water.

"It's biting! Pull!" Papa whispered excitedly.

I pulled. Oh, how heavy! The rod bent in a bow, while the line, stretched tight as a harp string, seemed to cut the water.

"Don't hurry or it will tear off!" worried Papa. "Let me help—you'll lose it, a big one has taken the bait."

But I clung to the rod with both hands and wouldn't give it up.

The powerful fish, stretching the line taut, threw itself from side to side. I couldn't pull it up to the bank. Finally the fish appeared out of the depths.

With all my strength I pulled on the rod. A light crack sounded, and in my hands was left a broken end. The other end, together with the float and line, was speeding swiftly on the water away from the bank.

"It's gone, it's gone!" I screamed, and forgetting everything in the world, dashed after the fleeing end right into the water.

Papa barely caught me by my jacket.

"You'll drown! It's deep here!"

But I saw nothing except the yellow bamboo end of my rod, which, cutting the water, was moving ever farther and farther away.

"It's gone, gone!" I repeated in dismay.

At my yells, my frightened Mamma came running. She had gone off to gather brushwood for a campfire.

"What happened?" she asked while yet at a distance.

"Don't cry," Papa comforted me. "Maybe we'll catch it yet."

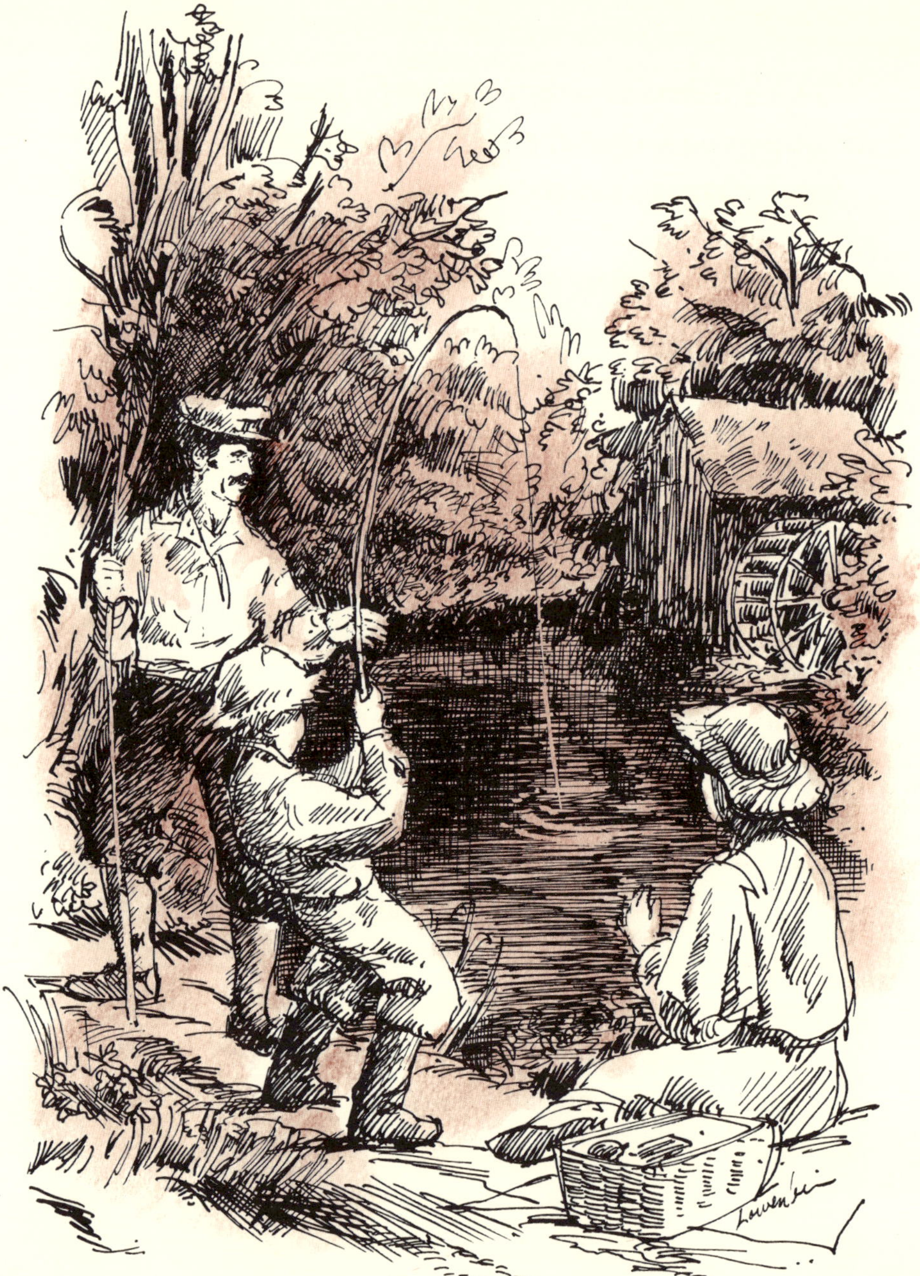

But I didn't believe him. Tears poured from my eyes, and it seemed to me that in all the world there was no more unfortunate being than I.

At last I calmed down a little.

Papa was standing on the bank and looking intently toward the opposite end of the pool.

"Dragged it to the bushes. If only it would come nearer the bank," he said.

I understood that not all was yet lost. And a timid hope stirred in my soul.

With my eyes, I, too, found the thin white stick, which barely showed on the water closer to the other bank. It was moving ever farther away.

"To the bushes, it's going to the bushes!" Papa joyfully repeated. "Cheer up, Ura. We'll pick it up yet!"

Mamma, too, was following the rod.

"Ah, if only it would approach the shore!"

At last the fish dragged the rod to the bushes.

At this all three of us—Papa, Mamma, and I—dashed across the dam to the other end of the pool.

Here now were the bushes. On the water near them, the broken end of the rod was gently rocking. And the float also calmly rocked on the water.

Maybe the rod was already empty? Perhaps the fish had long ago torn itself off?

Stealing up, Papa approached the bank, went knee-deep into the water and stretched his hand out to the rod . . . and suddenly it leaped up, as if alive, and rushed away. Papa went straight after it—plop—right into the water. All wet, he jumped out on the bank.

Oh joy, oh happiness! In his hands was the broken rod! It was bent in a bow, and the line, once more like a tight string, cut the water. The frightened fish pulled toward the depths and wouldn't come to the bank.

But Papa tried to overpower it. He would let the line out, then lightly draw it in again.

He was trying to tire the fish out. And Mamma and I, holding our breath, followed this struggle.

At last the exhausted fish appeared on the surface and even turned a little on its side, its silver scales sparkling.

Then Papa carefully passed me the bit of fishing rod:

"Pull, but gently, don't hurry."

I seized the rod in my hands and, forgetting everything in the world, pulled toward the bank with all my strength.

"Gently, gently, it'll break away!" cried Papa.

The fish rushed into the depths. I pulled toward myself.

In the grass on the bank something began to slap, to thrash around.

Papa and Mamma dashed there. And now again I felt a kind of lightness in my hands.

"It's torn off, it's gone!"

But at the same instant Papa threw far out on the bank a fish with glittering scales. It slapped heavily in the grass and thrashed around and leaped in it.

We ran up to our catch. In the grass, pressing down the green stalks, lay a large chub. I seized it in both hands and began to examine it with delight. Its back was dark green, almost black, its sides silver, and the head was big, broad.

"Well, I congratulate you. Now you are a real fisherman!" Mamma said joyfully.

"Yes, yes, a fisherman!" Papa laughed good-naturedly. "He almost lost it again. It had already torn itself off the hook. I just barely grabbed it in the grass."

"What do you want from him? Why, it's his first real catch," Mamma defended me. "And anyhow he pulled it out himself."

"Of course, of course," agreed Papa. "Let's go quickly to the fishing rods—maybe something has got on the hook without us."

He was wet and simply covered with mud, but he only squeezed his clothes a bit and gaily waved his hand, saying: "Never mind, by evening everything will be dry."

On one of our rods there actually was a big perch.

Papa gave me one of his own rods to take the place of my broken one and we continued to fish. But I didn't so much fish as run to the nearby bushes under which, in the thick grass, covered with burdock leaves against the sun, lay my chub. And how huge and handsome it seemed to me!

Mamma kept going to the chub, too, touching it with her hand, shaking her head, and smiling. Probably she rejoiced over my success no less than I did.

And Papa kept looking at me and saying:

"Well, brother, are you satisfied, eh?"

I felt I was the happiest human being alive.

I caught, besides, two ruff. And Papa caught many

different fish and even got a pike. As for Mamma, she lit a campfire on the bank, prepared dinner and tea, then fished with us, and pulled out a perch.

Finally, when it was already beginning to get dark, we prepared to go home. I wanted terribly not to go. It seemed as if I could have sat all summer here by the river, under the old white willows. But nothing could be done about it. We harnessed the horse and rode off for home.

Quail were calling loudly in the fields, as if saying: "Time to sleep, time to sleep!" Listening to them, I really did doze off for a bit. And all the time before my eyes the water rippled with the floats on it. . . .

Suddenly Mamma touched me on the shoulder:

"Look, Ura, look quickly."

I woke up. We were riding through a little birch wood. I looked into the depths where Mamma was pointing.

What was that? A tiny blue fire lit up in the dark night grass. And there, a little farther, another and another. Or was it the stars reflecting themselves in the drops of dew? No, that couldn't be. . . .

"See, fireflies," said Papa. He stopped the horse. "If you like, collect them into a box, and at home we'll let them out in the orchard. Let them live with us."

Mamma and I walked a long time on the thick, moist grass, looking for the tiny living stars. And overhead the dark branches of trees interwove, and in the gaps between, like fireflies, the far-off blue stars glittered.

And perhaps it was just then, on that happy day, that I suddenly felt with all my heart how fine our homeland nature is—and that there is none better in all the world.

The Tomtit

It was freezing hard outside. Every morning after breakfast I would put on my fur coat and felt boots and run out to play for a little while. I would run first of all to the apple tree in the orchard, where a month before Papa and I had built a birds' dining room.

I would put crumbs and seeds on a small plank and then go sliding on my sled down the hill. But the cold was usually so fierce that my face and hands began to freeze, and I had to return home.

At home I often ran to the window while playing and looked out to see what was going on outside. The trees in the orchard were gray with hoarfrost, and the sun shone dimly, as if through fog.

Ah, how cold it was for birds at liberty! They scarcely showed themselves. They hid from the penetrating, icy wind, somewhere under the eaves.

Once in the morning, when I ran out of the house to

carry food to the birds, I suddenly saw, dark against the fence, a little bunch of feathers of some sort. I went up to it.

Right on the snow lay a tomtit. It didn't move. Its eyes were closed.

I took the bird in my hands and tried to warm it with my breath. "Is it really all frozen?" I thought.

But then suddenly the tomtit opened its black, beady eyes and at once closed them again.

"It's alive, alive!" I thought with joy and ran home holding the bird in my hands.

Mamma and I laid the tomtit in a cage and set the cage as close as possible to the stove.

"What do you think, Mamma? Will it come to life?" I asked.

"I think it will warm up," she answered.

And suddenly the bird seemed to wake up. It opened its eyes, shook its wings, jumped up on its feet, and cheeped very loudly. Then it began to shake itself, preen itself, put its feathers in order.

Cautiously I put a little cup of hempseed and a saucer of water into the cage.

But the tomtit wasn't frightened of my hand. It only jumped lightly away to the other end of the cage, and when I took my hand out and locked the door, it immediately flew up to the edge of the cup and began to peck the hempseed.

"Look, Mamma, it's tame!" I cried happily.

"No, Ura, it's not tame, but very hungry. Right now, you know, birds have a hard time getting food for themselves."

"Then why don't they all fly to the dining room Papa and I built for them?"

"Because not all the birds know about your dining room. This one probably flew here from some far-off place," answered Mamma.

The tomtit ate its fill, drank water from the saucer, and began to jump from perch to perch.

I set the cage on the window sill in my bedroom and went about my affairs.

At dinner time Papa came home. He looked at the tomtit and said:

"It will live a couple of days in the cage, and then we can let it out. Let it fly about the rooms."

"And what if it flies out the door or through the window?" I worried. "It can get frozen again."

"No, now it won't perish from hunger and cold," answered Papa. "Tomtits are clever birds. Once we have fed it and warmed it here, it will keep close to our house all winter and will find your dining room in a jiffy."

"Then perhaps it would be better to let it out?" suggested Mamma.

But I hated to part so soon with this gay bird, and I said:

"Let it live a while with us, in the cage. It will warm itself, fatten up, and then in the spring we will let it out."

So the tomtit lived with us the whole winter long. It picked up very quickly, spent whole days jumping from perch to perch, and didn't beat against the bars when I set a cup of water for it or poured hempseed into its trough.

And one time the bird, unable even to wait till I put its food down, jumped, cheeping, right on my hand. It jumped along my hand once, twice, then stopped, bent its head and suddenly pecked me on a birthmark on my finger—pecked and even drew it lightly toward itself. But, convinced that this was not something to eat, the tomtit comically shook its head and then cleaned its beak against my hand.

I was delighted and kept my hand in the cage. The tomtit had become very familiar with it, apparently. It would now jump on my hand, now fly up to the perch.

At last I got tired of holding my hand in the same position, drew it out of the cage and went to call Mamma so that she should see how well I had tamed the bird. We were returning together when we saw Grandma coming out of the bedroom.

"Wait, Ura, don't go in," she stopped me. "I opened the window to air the room out a little."

Mamma went in, closed the window, and came back at once.

"Ura, don't get upset," she said. "You forgot to lock the cage. The tomtit isn't there—it flew out through the window."

I ran into my bedroom. I looked the whole room over—the tomtit wasn't anywhere.

"It's a good thing it flew away," said Mamma, trying to comfort me. "It is much better for your tomtit to be at liberty now than in the cage. No need to torment it for nothing."

"But if it had lived with us just a little longer . . ." I exclaimed unhappily. "Perhaps it would have become so used to me it wouldn't have wanted to fly away."

"Well, such things don't happen!" Mamma replied. "I am confident that it will settle somewhere near our house and it will build its nest here. We shall certainly see it again."

I believed Mamma and was quite comforted. And when Papa came home, he also said:

"It's a good thing you let the tomtit out. Soon it will be spring. It has to build a nest, not sit in a cage."

We were talking in the dining room where Mamma was setting the table for dinner and I was helping her.

Suddenly it seemed to me that Mamma gently tapped her finger against a plate.

"Why are you doing that?" I asked her.

She didn't understand.

"Why did you tap on the plate?"

"I didn't even think of tapping!"

"But who, then . . ."

I hadn't finished speaking when the gentle tapping sounded again.

"Do you hear, do you hear?"

The tapping was again repeated.

"It's in your bedroom—someone is tapping at the window," said Mamma.

She looked in, then at once raising her fingers, whispered:

"Sh-sh-sh . . . quiet, quiet."

Papa and I went up to the door on tiptoe and also looked in. On the sill outside the window sat the tomtit. At one moment it looked into the room, the next it tapped with its beak against the glass—apparently it was trying to fly into the room and couldn't.

Mamma cautiously went up to the window, but she had only stretched her hand to open it when the tomtit took wing and disappeared.

"It flew away—now it won't fly back again!" I was all upset.

"We don't know that," said Papa. "Leave the window open and let's eat, for I'm very hungry."

At dinner I hardly ate anything and all the time kept listening—maybe the tomtit would cheep in the next room. Several times I even tried to jump from the table, but Mamma said sternly:

"Until you eat up your soup and second course, I won't let you leave the table."

I had to eat up everything.

When at last this endless dinner was over, I ran to the door and looked into the bedroom. The cage stood empty on the window sill, and the tomtit was nowhere to be seen.

I sat down by the window in the dining room and began to leaf through a book with pictures in it. But all the time I was thinking about the tomtit. . . . If we hadn't closed the window at once, the tomtit would have returned to us. And now it had flown somewhere far away and would never come back.

At last Mamma, too, said it looked as if the tomtit didn't want to come back. Anyway it was time to close the window, since we had cooled off the whole room. She went in, and having locked the window, opened the door so the temperature would get even.

A little later I went in to clean up the empty cage. As I passed the window, I glanced outside. Half rain, half snow was falling. Under the window the snowdrifts had settled and become quite dark, and the wet, bare trees in the orchard also looked uninvitingly dark.

"Cheerivik!" sounded loudly and distinctly somewhere close beside me. I started and looked around.

"Cheerivik!" sounded again. I raised my head. On the edge of the dresser sat the tomtit casting glances down at me.

"Mamma! It's here, here!" I cried joyfully.

Everybody—Mamma, Papa, and Grandma—ran into the room and at once saw the tomtit.

"How did I fail to notice it when I went in to close the window?" asked Mamma.

"And I, too, didn't notice it at once!" I said happily. "It saw me first and greeted me!"

"Well, now leave it alone," said Papa. "When it wants to, it will fly into the cage of its own accord."

And, indeed, after flying a little about the room, the tomtit flew into its cage and began to peck hungrily at the hempseed. Then it flew out again and seated itself on a corner of the stove. It was already evening. Puffed up like a little ball, the tomtit hid its head under its wing and fell asleep like that, sitting on the stove.

From that time on, it lived with us in full freedom.

A Present

No matter who came to see us, they all said our house was a real zoo. We had birds living in a room, a squirrel, and a tame hedgehog—we called him Zluchka-Kaluchka (Vicious Pricker).

And once in the wintertime I brought Papa a remarkable present. I found it with my chum Kostya.

We were walking in the forest behind the village.

We saw an old stump, all moldy, and began to break it up.

Suddenly, Kostya bent down:

"Look, Ura, what's that?"

I bent down, too. I looked—in the middle of the stump, right in the mold, something shone like gold. Some kind of ring. Only a big one, like a bracelet.

Kostya said:

"Can it be hidden treasure?"

He picked it up—and suddenly he threw it!

"A snake! Don't touch it!" he yelled.

But the snake had fallen on the snow and didn't move.

We took sticks, began to stir it up, but it didn't uncoil.

Kostya even picked it up on a stick. The snake didn't stir there either.

"So then," we thought, "it's dead." I touched it with my finger—it was hard, all dried out.

Kostya said:

"This is a grass snake. When it's alive, it's terrible. If it stings you, you die."

And I said:

"It's not true that it stings. Papa told me—snakes don't sting, they bite. They don't have any sting, but they have teeth, and in their teeth are little sacs with poison in them. When a snake bites, it lets the poison out of the sac into the wound."

"That's not important—stings or bites," said Kostya. "Anyway you'll die."

We took the dead snake in our hands and began to examine it: it was so handsome—it shone as if it were made of copper.

Papa had not told me anything about snakes like that. He had told me about adders—gray ones and black. They bite and are poisonous. But grass snakes are not poisonous and don't bite. They only hiss and quickly-quickly stick out their little tongue. He who doesn't know thinks that this isn't a tongue but a sting and is afraid.

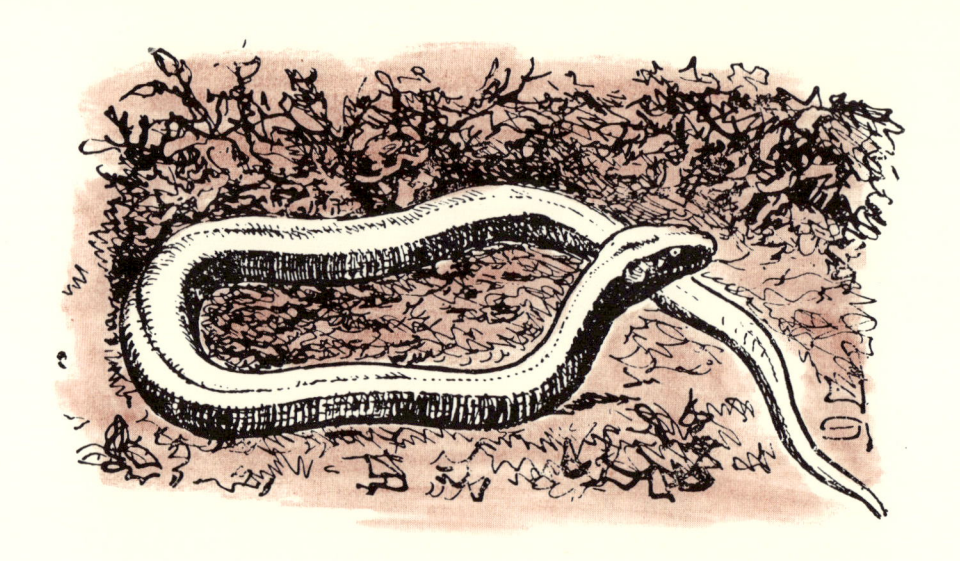

But I was not afraid. You can tell a grass snake from an adder very simply, because on its head it has two small yellow spots, and on an adder there aren't any such spots.

Grass snakes and adders I knew, but this kind of snake I was seeing for the first time.

I asked Kostya to give it to me.

He agreed. Only he said that I should give him some fish hooks.

I put the snake in my pocket and ran home. I wanted to show it to Papa at once. But at home Mamma said that Papa had gone to see some sick people in another village and would come home quite late.

Then I decided to make a surprise for him: I laid the snake on his writing-table beside the inkwell and covered it with a blotter so that Mamma wouldn't see it beforehand and throw it out. Papa would arrive, start to write something—and would find my present.

So I arranged it and went out for a stroll.

When they called me to dinner, I looked into Papa's study first thing. I opened the door, I looked—the blotter was lying on the floor and there was no snake.

I went to Mamma:

"Why did you throw away the present I put on Papa's table?"

"What present? I didn't take anything from Papa's table."

I was confused. I kept quiet and thought to myself: "Did the snake run away by itself? Then it's not dead but was only pretending?"

I was terrified. Why, it was poisonous! And suppose it bit us all now?

I didn't say anything to anybody. I put on my father's leather gauntlets and began to look for the snake. All day I crawled under chairs, looked under cupboards, but nowhere did I find it. Only our hedgehog—Zluchka-Kaluchka—was sleeping rolled up in a ball on some warm slippers under the bed.

He always slept there. And Mamma was very cross with him about it. She would want her slippers, would stick her foot under the bed—and suddenly he would jump up and prick her on the foot, and even snort that people shouldn't disturb him!

I rummaged through all the rooms, got worn out, but didn't find the snake. "So," I thought, "it crawled out of some chink or other and got away from the house." Just the same I was a little frightened. What if it had hidden somewhere and was sitting, waiting?

In the evening Mamma went into the hall for something and suddenly she cried out:

"Oh, what's that?"

I jumped out of the room and ran straight to Mamma.

I looked—she had climbed on a chair and was staring at the floor, where our Zluchka-Kaluchka was catching at something and pulling it about. Just then the outside door opened and Papa came in.

"What's going on?" he asked.

Mamma pointed to the floor:

"A snake, a snake!"

Papa ran up, bent over, seized the hedgehog, and began to take the snake away from him.

I saw my snake, quite alive, turning in Papa's hands and catching at his fingers.

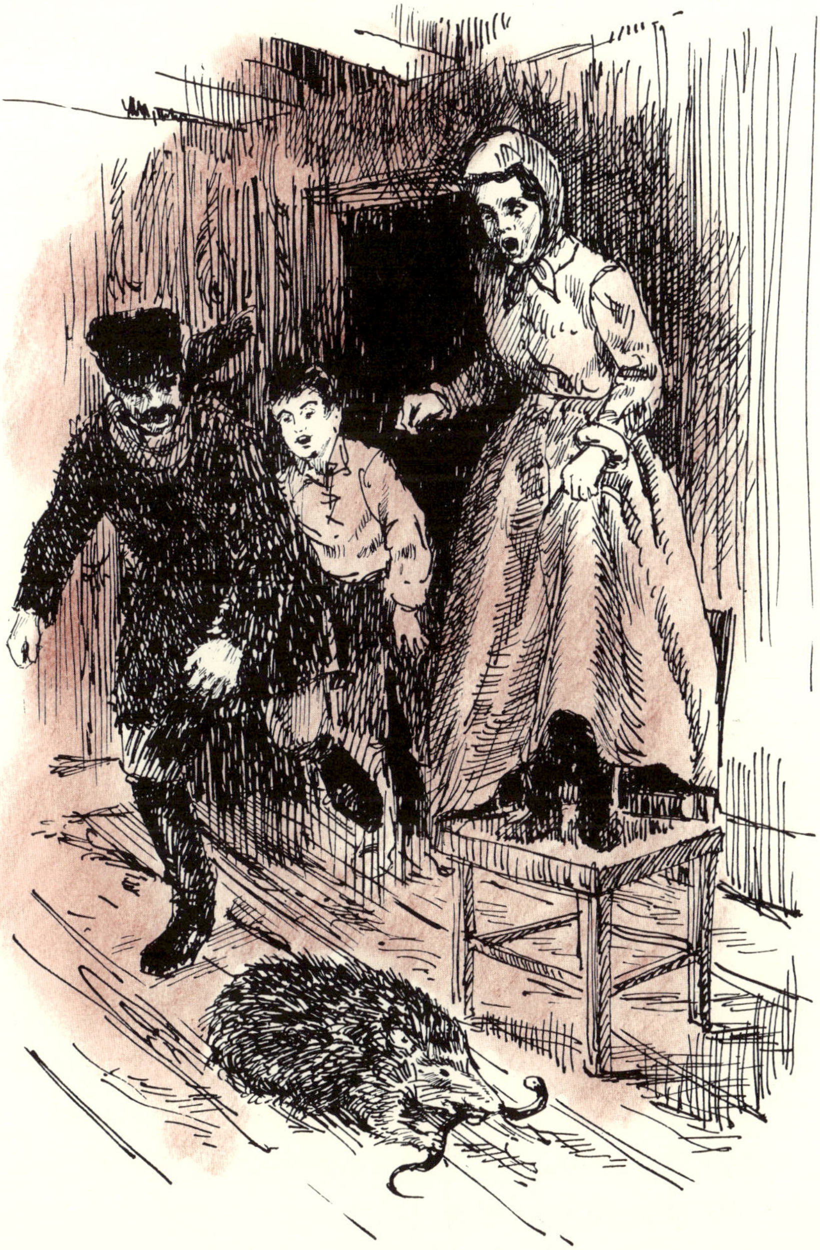

"Drop it, drop it!" I screamed. "That's a snake! It's poisonous!"

But Papa started to laugh and said:

"What are you making a noise for? This isn't a snake at all but a lizard, only without legs."

I didn't believe it.

"Where did it put its legs, then?"

"Didn't put them anywhere," said Papa. "There is such a lizard, and it is called a blindworm. It isn't at all poisonous."

Here I suddenly stopped being afraid, ran up to Papa and began asking him to put the blindworm in a jar.

But Mamma wouldn't hear of it.

"Take away this filth," she said. "I shan't allow it to be kept in the house anyway."

Papa carried the blindworm off to his study and called me to go with him.

"This is very surprising," he said. "How could a blindworm get into our house in winter?"

Then I told him everything: how I had brought it from the forest and laid it on his table. And it wasn't dead but was only pretending.

"It wasn't pretending but sleeping very soundly," Papa explained to me. " 'Way back in the fall it got into the moldy stump and then fell asleep for the whole winter. All snakes and blindworms seem to act like that."

Papa got a jar, put some paper in it, then set our lizard there, and tied the jar up with cheesecloth and carried it away to a closet. He said that the blindworm would fall asleep again in the cold and would sleep till spring. And in the spring, as soon as the sun warmed it up, it would wake up and we would let it out into the forest.

That's how it was. The blindworm fell asleep in the jar in our house and slept through the whole winter.

We forgot all about it, and in the spring, when we remembered, we looked—but the jar was empty. So it must have been that it woke up and crawled out one day. Probably the jar was poorly tied.

When Mamma found out that the blindworm had gone off again, she was frightened and got very angry at Papa and me.

Long after that, every evening before going to bed she would look under all the chairs, under the beds, behind dressers, all the time grumbling at us, saying that we would probably soon drag a crocodile into the house.

And, to tell the truth, at that time I wanted very much to acquire a crocodile, even the very smallest.

A Thoughtful Mamma

Once the shepherds caught a fox cub somehow and brought him to us. We put the little animal in an empty storehouse.

The fox cub was very small yet, all gray, with a dark little muzzle and a white tip to his tail. The creature hid in the farthest corner of the storehouse and looked about him. He was so frightened that he didn't even bite when we stroked him, only pressed his ears close and trembled all over.

Mamma poured some milk into a little bowl for him and set it right beside him. But the frightened little beast wouldn't drink the milk.

Then Papa said we had to leave the fox cub in peace —let him look around, let him get used to the new place.

I didn't want to go away in the least, but Papa locked the door and we went home.

That night I woke up. Somewhere quite close by I thought I heard a puppy yelping. "Where," I thought, "did he come from?" I looked out of the window. Outside, day was already breaking. From the window I could see the storehouse where the fox cub was. That's who was whining like a pup, it seemed.

Right behind the storehouse the forest began.

Suddenly I saw a fox jump out of the bushes, stop, listen, and stealing along, run up to the storehouse. At once the yelping stopped, and instead of it there sounded a joyous whine.

I quietly woke up Mamma and Papa, and we all began looking out of the window together.

The fox was running around the barn and trying to dig up the earth under it. But there was a strong stone foundation—the fox couldn't do anything. Pretty soon she ran off into the bushes, and the fox cub began to yelp again.

I wanted to watch for the fox all night, but Papa said she wouldn't come any more and make me go to sleep.

I woke up late and quickly dressing, hurried off first thing to visit the fox cub. What was this? On the threshold lay a little dead rabbit.

I ran just as fast as I could to Papa and brought him back with me.

"What do you know!" said Papa, seeing the little rabbit. "So the mother fox came once more and brought food for the fox cub. She couldn't get inside, so she left it outside. Well, what a thoughtful Mamma!"

All day long I fidgeted around the barn, looking through the chinks. Twice I went in with Mamma to feed the fox cub. And in the evening I couldn't fall asleep, but kept jumping out of bed all the time and looking through the window—maybe the fox had come.

Finally Mamma got angry and hung a dark curtain over the window.

To make up for it, I got up at daybreak and at once ran to the barn. This time there lay on the threshold not a little rabbit, but a neighbor's smothered hen. Evidently the fox had come again in the night to visit her cub. She hadn't succeeded in catching game in the forest, so she climbed into our neighbor's hen house, stifled a hen, and brought it to her young one.

Papa had to pay for the hen, and we got soundly bawled out by our neighbor besides.

"Take that fox cub away any place you like!" he shouted. "Otherwise the fox will steal all our poultry!"

Nothing could be done. Papa was obliged to put the fox cub in a bag and carry him back into the forest, to the fox dens.

After that the fox didn't come into the village any more.

Baby Storks

We lived in the Ukraine one year, in a small settlement, amidst far-stretching cherry orchards.

Not far from our house grew an old tree. And early in the spring it happened once that a stork flew up and settled on it. For a long time it looked something over, clumsily stepping on its long legs along a thick bough. Then it flew away.

But next morning we saw that there were already two storks bustling about on the tree. They were building a nest.

Soon the nest was ready. The female stork laid eggs there and began to sit on them. And the male stork now flew to the marsh for food, now stood near the nest on the bough, with one leg tucked up under him. In this way, on one leg, he could stand a very long time, and could even doze a little.

When the baby storks hatched out, great cares began

for the old storks. The nestlings were big gluttons. All day long they demanded food, and from morning to evening, turn and turn about, the parent storks dragged frogs, little fishes, and lizards for them from the marsh.

While one of the storks flew after food, the other stood on the edge of the nest, guarding the nestlings. As soon as it saw the second stork flying up to the nest, it would tilt its head back and loudly clap its beak, just like a rattle. For storks have no call. They welcome one another by clicking their beaks very fast.

The bird that had arrived gave its catch to the young and sat down by the nest to rest, while the other stork immediately flew off to the marsh to hunt for frogs.

In this way, turn and turn about, the storks fed the nestlings the whole day long. And when they grew up a little and became still more gluttonous, both parents began to fly together to get food for the young.

Another week and a half passed, and suddenly one of the stork parents disappeared. What happened to it was unknown—perhaps it was killed, or perhaps it perished in some way by itself.

What a hard time began now for the stork that was left! The nestlings had already grown quite big. There were three of them, and they demanded a great deal of food.

As soon as dawn appeared, the stork was already hurrying off to the marsh for its catch, would bring it, shove it into the mouth of one of the nestlings and, without resting a minute, would fly back to the hunt.

Thus it toiled till late in the evening.

We were very sorry for the poor bird, but we didn't know how to help it.

Once we went to the river to catch fish. As we were coming home, we saw all three baby storks stretching their long necks out of the nest, opening their beaks, and asking for food. And the stork was not by the nest. It was catching frogs on the marsh, apparently.

"What if we tried to feed them some fish?" proposed my chum.

In a twinkling we climbed the tree. Seeing us, the baby storks got excited, fidgeted, and almost fell out of the nest.

But then one of them noticed a little fish in my hand. The baby bird stretched toward it, grabbed it with its beak, and swallowed it. The others immediately followed its example.

We gave the baby storks all our fish, climbed down from the tree, and only then saw the old stork. It hastily flew to the nest and began looking it over in a worried way, to see if everything was all right there.

After that we began to feed the baby storks every day. We caught fish and frogs especially for them.

The baby storks quickly understood what was what. No sooner did we climb the tree than they all stretched their long necks out of the nest toward us and opened their mouths, begging us to feed them.

At last our nurselings quite grew up. They got covered with feathers and began to fly out of the nest. And now they simply wouldn't let us alone—the baby storks would not let us pass by. We needed only to appear outdoors and they would fly down from the nest and rush headlong to us, demanding food.

And the grown-up stork seemed to understand that things would be managed without it—more and more rarely did it bring food for the babies. A large part of the day it either wandered along the marsh, eating frogs, or dozed on the tree by the nest. In the meantime the baby storks chased after us in the yard, demanding food.

Once they insisted on going with us to the marsh. There were many frogs there. The baby storks began to catch them themselves and forgot all about us. After that day, they flew to the marsh every morning to hunt for frogs.

The summer ended. All the storks were gathering in flocks, preparing to fly away. Ours also stopped spending the night on the tree by the nest. Doubtless they had attached themselves to some flock or other, and we had already begun to forget our nurselings.

But once we were on our way home from fishing when we saw a flock of storks strolling about on the meadow. They noticed us, got on the alert—in a moment they would fly off. Suddenly we saw three storks separate themselves from the flock and come straight toward us.

"Why, those are our baby storks!" we cried joyfully and began to entice them with fish.

And those big wild birds ran up to us, began flapping their wings and bustling around—they simply snatched the fish from our hands!

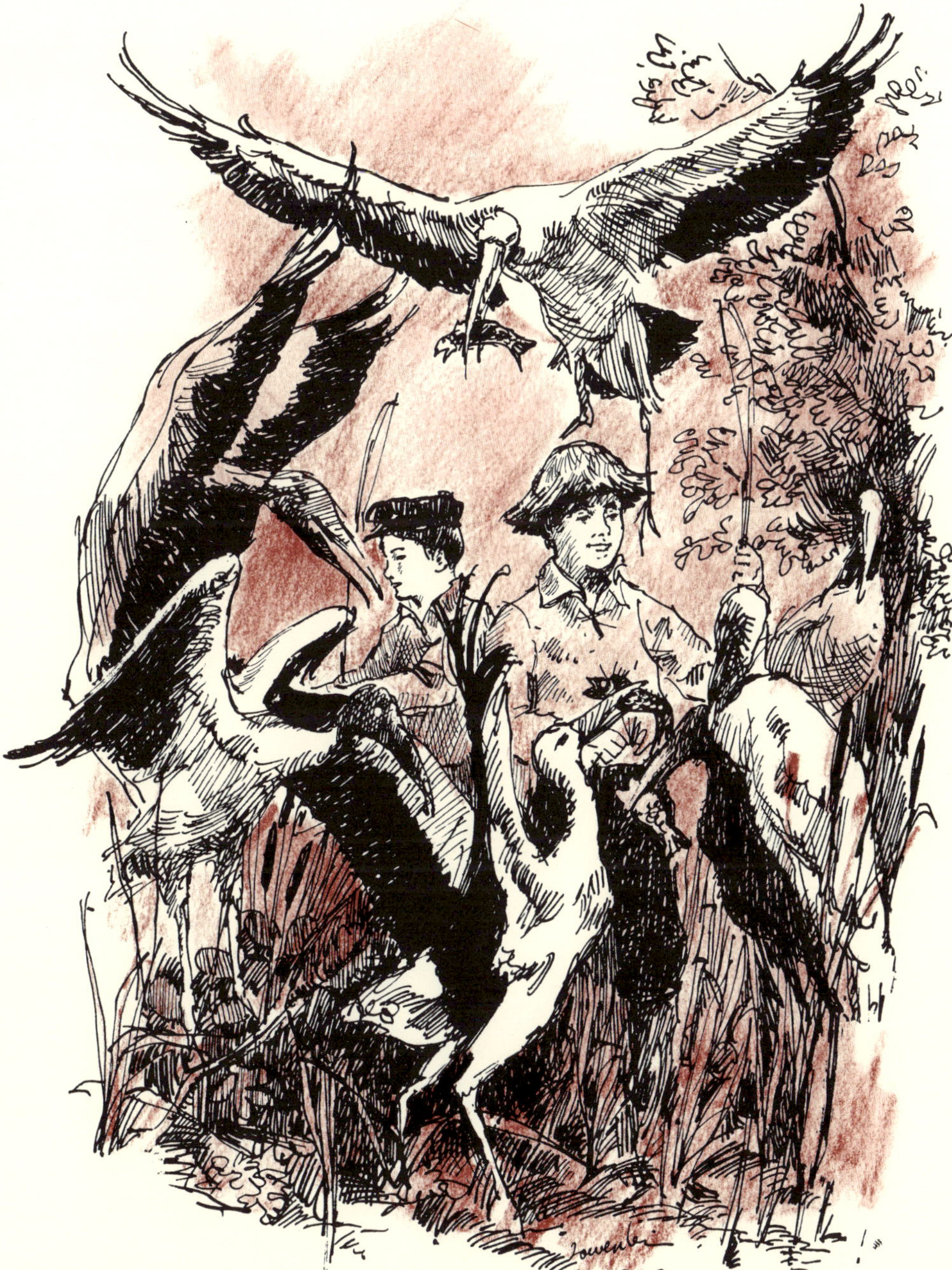

A stork would grab a little fish, throw it up in the air, catch it again more comfortably, and swallow it, and then tilt its head back and rattle its beak with delight.

Our storks were eating fish out of our hands, and the whole flock was watching from a distance. They stretched out their necks, they looked—it was clear they couldn't understand it.

The storks ate their fill, clapped their beaks in gratitude, and went back to the flock. And we went home.

We didn't see them any more. It got cold, and they flew off to the warm south.

Longears

I began hunting very early. When I was twelve years old, Papa made me a present of a gun and began to take me with him to the forest and the marsh.

Once in autumn we were returning from a hunt. I climbed down from the cart and walked beside it to stretch my legs. We were going through a small forest just then. The whole road was covered with leaves. Suddenly I saw something dark lying on the road among the leaves. I bent down, I looked—a baby rabbit, and what a little one! I was amazed—the cart had just gone over this spot. How was it that it hadn't crushed the rabbit?

"Well," I said, "it's clear, bunny, you're a lucky fellow."

I took him up in my hands, and he huddled up on my palm, sat and trembled, but didn't try to run away. "I'll take him home," I thought. "Maybe he'll live, and here he'll perish anyway—he was born very late. Soon winter will come on. He'll freeze, poor thing, or become breakfast for a fox."

I spread some leaves in my hunter's bag, set the little rabbit there, and brought him home.

At home Mamma poured some milk into a saucer and gave it to the bunny. Only he wouldn't drink—he was too small yet, he didn't know how. We took a little bottle, poured milk into it, put a nipple on the bottle and gave it to the little rabbit. He smelled the nipple, moved his whiskers. Mamma squeezed a drop of milk from the nipple and smeared the bunny's nose with it. He licked it off, half opened his mouth, and we stuck the end of the nipple in. The baby rabbit began to smack his lips, sucked, and drank up the whole bottle.

The bunny got used to us. He jumped through the rooms and wasn't afraid of anybody.

A month passed, another, a third. . . . Our rabbit grew up, became quite big, and we named him Longears. He settled down to live under the stove. When he was frightened of anything he'd go straight there.

Besides Longears, there lived with us our old cat Ivanich and our hunting dog Jack.

Ivanich and Jack were the greatest of friends. They ate together out of the same dish and even slept together. Jack had a rug on the floor. In wintertime, when it got cold in the house, Ivanich would join Jack on the rug and roll up in a ball. Jack would at once go to him—he'd stick his nose right in Ivanich's belly and warm his muzzle. And he himself breathed so warm, so warm that Ivanich also was satisfied.

When the rabbit appeared in the house, Ivanich didn't pay any attention to him, and Jack at first looked at him with an unfavorable eye, but quickly got used to him. And after that, all three became very good friends.

It was especially nice in the evenings, when the stove was heated. At once all of them came to the fire to warm themselves. They would sit down very close to one another and would look into the stove.

It would be dark in the room, only red gleams running along the walls, and after them black shadows. And for this reason it seemed that everything in the room—tables, chairs—were moving as if they were alive. The wood burned, burned, and suddenly—crackle—out would fly a golden bit of coal. Then the friends would get away from the stove, scatter in all directions. They'd jump away and look at one another as if asking: "What happened?" And afterwards little by little they would calm down—and again to the fire.

Or they would organize play. It always began like this. Here they are lying all three together, dozing. Suddenly Ivanich catches at Longears gently with his paw, touches him once, twice. The rabbit lies, lies, then suddenly jumps up and starts to run, Ivanich after him, Jack after Ivanich, and that way one after another through all the rooms. And when the rabbit gets tired of it, he marches under the stove, and that's the end of the play.

And before lying down to sleep, Longears would tangle up his tracks. Rabbits always do that when they live in freedom. If you look at a rabbit's tracks on the snow, you won't be able to figure out where the little creature went. Not for naught are such tracks called "rabbits' loops." A hunting dog stumbles on them—while he is figuring them out, going here and there along the tracks, the rabbit has long ago run away.

So our Longears, every day before crawling under the stove, also tried to tangle up his tracks. He would jump backward and forward through the room, making his rabbits' loops, while right there on the rug the hunting dog Jack dozed and looked at him with one eye as if he were laughing at the foolish rabbit.

Thus Longears lived through the whole winter with us. Spring came, friendly and warm. Scarcely had we turned around when the grass was already getting green. We decided to let Longears out into the forest, to go free. I put him in a basket, went to the forest, and took Jack with me—to let him see his friend off. I wanted to put Ivanich in the basket, too, so that he should see him off also, but it was very heavy to carry. So I left him at home.

We came to the forest. I took Longears out of the basket and put him down on the grass. But he didn't know what to do next, didn't run, just moved his ears. I clapped my hands:

"Run into the forest, bunny! What are you sitting here for?"

Longears got frightened and went hopping into the forest, with Jack after him.

"There," I thought, "it's better to chase each other in the bushes than in the rooms."

I waited—Jack didn't come back. Only suddenly I heard a rabbit's cry in the forest, again and again . . . I dashed toward the cry, ran up. I looked—and Jack already had Longears in his teeth.

I shouted:

"Drop him! What are you doing? Why, that's our Longears!"

And Jack looked at me and wagged his tail, as if he wanted to say: "I caught a beast for you, and you are scolding me."

Clearly, Jack didn't recognize Longears in the forest and seized him as he would a wild rabbit.

I took Longears away, set him down on the grass, while I held Jack by the collar and didn't let him go.

Here the bunny doubtless realized that in the forest you can't play with a dog. He laid his ears back and marched into the bushes. That's the last Jack and I saw of him.

The Draw

One Saturday night Papa said that we would go snipe hunting next day—to the draw, of course—if only the weather was fair. Oh, how I wanted it to be fair!

I woke up early. I looked out the window—sun, not a cloud in the sky. So—we were going.

Papa and I began to fill our cartridge belts, cleaned our guns once more, and greased our boots. By dinner time everything was ready. We ate our dinner—and off to the forest.

You have to go to the draw toward evening. The snipe are to be found there in the spring after sunset. As soon as the sun goes down and twilight comes on, the long-nosed forest cocks—snipe—begin to fly over glade and grove. Each one is looking for a mate. And the snipe hens meantime are sitting somewhere in the glades. The males go looking for them in the evening glow, as they fly over the forest. In hunters' language this is called the draw. All this I knew long ago from Papa, only I had never yet seen a draw.

We came to the place long before sunset. Roundabout was half-grown forest, young birches, aspens. All of them were in blossom, all with long catkins. And if you looked into the distance, the trees seemed to be in a greenish fog. That was the leaves already coming out.

On the ground, from under last year's leaves, young grass stuck out. And in the low places near the spring puddles, the grass was already high, green, and the first yellow flowers had opened.

We chose an open glade. Papa said:

"Well, we'll stand here for the draw. And we aren't a bit late. You were worrying and sighing all for nothing. Stand there in that corner under the little birch and listen. When a snipe flies, he keeps piping all the time like this: 'Tzik-tzik, tzik-tzik. . . .' And then he says, 'Khor-khor, khor-khor. . . .' You'll hear him when he is yet far off. Only look well, don't gape."

Papa took his stand at one end of the glade and I at the other.

The sun had already begun to sink, big, red, quite without rays, like a red balloon. A breeze came up, and the air began to smell of greenery. I took a deep breath while I kept looking, kept listening, so as not to miss the snipe. And all around the birds were singing at the top of their voices, whistling, cheeping, especially the thrushes. Toward evening they raised such a din, I was afraid we wouldn't hear the snipe on account of them!

Then, when twilight fell, all the birds began little by little to quiet down. Only one thrush seated himself high, high up on the very tip of a fir tree and sang away. Finally he, too, became silent. And all at once it grew very still in the forest. A little bird of some kind cheeped in the bushes and then kept still. Only the frogs croaked in some puddle.

It was almost dark.

"Well," I thought, "so today we won't see any snipe!" And just as I thought that, suddenly I heard: "Tzik-tzik,

tzik-tzik." I grabbed my gun. I looked—a bird was flying over the forest, flying slowly and whistling. It passed by like that. You couldn't fire—it was far away. Oh, what bad luck!

Then someone else in the forest fired. But the snipe didn't fly toward us. I was quite crestfallen. And then suddenly again I heard: "Tzik-tzik, tzik-tzik." It was already near. And then—"Khor-khor, khor-khor . . ." I turned my head in every direction—I couldn't make out where he was flying. Then I saw that he had already passed right over my head and was flying directly toward Papa, flapping his wings occasionally, his long bill hanging down. I got so confused that I was too late to fire.

But now from the other end of the glade where Papa was standing—fire, a shot. The snipe seemed to stumble in the air and—dropped in a lump to the ground. I started running as fast as I could. And Papa, too, ran up. We began to search on the ground, in the bushes. We looked, looked—he wasn't anywhere. It was just as if the earth had opened and swallowed him up! We felt so disappointed. Papa even sighed.

"No," he said, "we won't find him. It seems he is wounded, he ran away."

"Let's stay here till morning," I proposed. "In the morning, when it's light, we'll find him without fail."

Papa only motioned with his hand as if to say: "Don't talk nonsense!" And he went off to the glade.

And I, too, was about to go with him. Only when I raised my head and looked—what was that hanging in the branches of the tree right next to me? I went up—it was the snipe. In falling, he had got caught on the branches and was left hanging there.

"Papa, Papa, come here!" I cried.

Papa ran up.

"Look," I said, "there he is!"

How glad Papa was!

"Good lad!" he said. "He's yours. I would never have found him."

"And yours, too. Why, *you* shot him."

"Well," Papa replied, "both of ours. So then, congratulations!"

We shook hands.

Then we went home as fast as we could. And I carried the snipe in my knapsack. That's how we had agreed.

My First Trophy

In early spring Papa and I went to hunt drakes on the nearest river. In summer this river is not at all wide and is all overgrown along the banks with old white willows and osier bushes. One bank is hilly, while the other is open meadowland. When you looked from the hill on the meadows beyond the river, you could see far, far all around. In places among the meadows, hillocks rose— narrow, long, like ridges, all of them overgrown with bushes. And among the hillocks glistened small lakes. In summer the meadows, the shrubbery, and the white willows on the banks—everything was green, and in the midst of this greenery the river itself wound like a narrow blue snake. And now, in the spring, in floodtime, everything was so changed you couldn't recognize it.

When Papa and I came out of the village onto a hillock, I looked and I didn't believe my eyes. No river, no meadows—there was nothing. Before us, continuous, many-colored water sparkled in the sun. A regular sea! This was our river spread so wide that you could hardly see the other shore, only in the distance the forests showed blue. And all over the flood, the hillocks overgrown with bushes could be seen like islands.

We hired a boat from some fishermen, put the basket with our decoy duck on a seat, sat down ourselves, and went off on the flood.

How nice it was all around! The sun shone so bright, so bright—it was even hot. The water was still, it didn't ripple anywhere. White gulls circled over the flood, sat down on the water, flew up again. . . .

We rowed to one of the little islands. On its shore Papa had already built a blind out of thick pine branches. I didn't realize at once that it was a blind—I thought it was a big juniper bush growing on the banks.

Papa hid the boat deep in the bushes, then took our tame duck out of the basket and let her swim on the water near the blind. And so that she shouldn't swim away, he tied her to a peg by a rope around her leg. Then he stuck the peg in the water so that neither it nor the rope could be seen on top of the water—it looked as if the duck were swimming in perfect freedom.

Papa and I crept into the blind and began to wait—maybe a wild drake would fly up to our duck.

In front of the blind, right by the water, grew a thin little aspen. Papa said:

"You see the aspen? If a drake sits down to the left of it, on your side, you fire, and if on the right, I will."

So we agreed, became silent, and began to wait.

It is very interesting to observe from a blind what is going on round about. Through the gaps between the branches you see everything, and behind the branches you yourself can't be seen.

We sat a little while. Suddenly a snipe flew right up to the blind. It sat down on the shore and began sticking its long bill into the soft earth to get worms.

Then a crow flew down, drank from the river, and began to bathe, splash, spatter.

For a long time Papa and I sat in the blind. The sun had already begun to slant toward the flood—a long golden path stretched from it over the water. I got bored sitting. I already wanted to ask Papa to take me for a ride in the boat.

I had just opened my mouth when suddenly our duck started to screech: "Ka-a-ka-ka-ka-ka! Ka-a-ka-ka-ka-ka!" She flapped her wings on the water, even cowered somehow. And at the same time I heard:

"Shvark-shvark, shvark-shvark...."

I held my breath. I already knew from Papa that this was a wild drake calling like that. I got my gun ready and looked at the duck through a gap. And she kept on screeching, flapping her wings on the water all the while. I looked—a handsome drake had flown right to her and sat down on the water.

Trakch! I fired my gun at him. Nothing could be seen, only smoke along the water. The smoke scattered. I looked again—and my dead drake was floating on the water. I leaped out of the blind and straight into the water—fortunately it was shallow!

Papa called out:

"Quiet, quiet! Don't frighten the duck!"

I got the drake and carried it to Papa. He laughed.

"You," he said, "are supposed to pay a fine."

"A fine for what?"

"For breaking our agreement. On which side of the aspen did the drake sit down—mine or yours?"

I had forgotten all about the aspen. Who thinks about aspens when a drake is right there! Why, this was my first hunting trophy!